BE HERE NOW

D1081164

Wise Publications
London / New York / Sydney / Paris / Copenhagen / Madrid

D'You Know What I Mean?

Words & Music by Noel Gallagher

1.Step off the train all a-lone at dawn, back in-to the hole where I___ was born,___ the
(Verses 2 & 3 see block lyric)

sun in the sky nev-er raised an eye— to me.—

The

blood on the trax and they must be mine, the fool on the hill and I— feel fine,—

don't look back 'cause you know what you might see.—

3

D.%. al Coda

Coda

All my peo-ple right here, right now, they know what I mean, yeah,

yeah. All my peo-ple right here, right now, they know what I mean,

yeah, yeah. All my peo-ple right here, right now,

All my peo - ple right here, right now, ___ d'you know what I mean, ___ yeah,

yeah. ___ All my peo - ple right here, right now, ___ d'you know what I mean, ___

___ yeah, yeah. ___ All my peo - ple right here, right now, ___

___ d'you know what I mean, ___ yeah, yeah, ___ yeah,

Verse 2:

Look into the wall of my mind's eye
I think I know but I don't know why
The questions are the answers you might need.
Coming in a mess going out in style
I ain't good looking but I'm someone's child
No one can give me the air that's mine to breathe.

Verse 3:

I don't really care for what you believe
So open up your fist or you won't receive
The thoughts and the words of everyman you'll need.
So gct up off thc floor and believe in life
No one's ever gonna ever ask you twice
Get on the bus and bring it on home to me.

My Big Mouth

Words & Music by Noel Gallagher

1. Ev - 'ry - bo - dy

knows
(Verse 2 see block lyric)

but no - one's say - ing noth - ing,

it was a sound so ve - ry loud that no - one can hear.—

— I got some - thing in my shoes,

you could fly a plane.___ I'll put on___ my shoes___

___ while I'm walk - ing slow - ly down the hall___ of fame,___ slow -

To Coda ⊕ |1.

- ly down the hall___ of fame.___

|2.

I ain't nev - er spoke to ___

Slow - ly down the hall— of fame.—

Solo ad lib.

1 - 3.

4.   *D.℅. al Coda*   ⊕ *Coda*

And round—   ——   Slow - ly down the hall—— of fame..

Slow - ly down the hall___ of fame.___

Verse 2:
I ain't ever spoke to God
And I ain't ever been to heaven
But you assumed I knew the way
Even though the map was given
And as you look into the eyes
Of a bloody cold assassin
It's only then you'll realise
With who's life you have been messin'.

And round this town *etc.*

Stand By Me

Words & Music by Noel Gallagher

1. Made a meal— and threw it up—
(Verses 2 & 3 see block lyric)

—— on Sun - day, I've—— got a lot of things— to learn.——

Said I would and I'll be leav-ing one— day, be - fore my heart starts to burn.—

So what's the mat - ter with you?—

Sing me some-thing new,— don't you know— the cold— and wind and rain don't know, they

on - ly seem to come and go— a - way.

1.

Stand by — me, — no - bo - dy knows, —

— yeah no - bo - dy knows —

the way it's gon - na · be. —

The way it's gon - na be, —

no - bo - dy knows,_____ yeah, God on - ly knows____

_____ the way it's gon - na be.____

Verse 2:
Times are hard when things have got no meaning
I've found a key upon the floor
Maybe you and I will not believe in
The things we find behind the door.

So what's the matter *etc.*

Verse 3:
If you're leaving will you take me with you
I'm tired of talking on my phone
There is one thing I can never give you
My heart will never be your home.

So what's the matter *etc.*

Magic Pie

Words & Music by Noel Gallagher

Vocal tacet 1 & 2°
You see me,— I've got— my mag - ic pie.—

28

Think of me,— yeah that was me I was— that pass - er - by.—

Repeat ad lib.

— I've been and now— I've gone.—

Verse 3:
There are but a thousand days
Preparing for a thousand years
Many minds to educate
The people who have disappeared
Do you dig my friends? Do you dig my shoes?
I am like a child with nothin' to lose
But my mind.
Yeah my mind
We'll have our way
In our own time
We'll have our say
'Cos my star's gonna shine

'Cos you see me *etc.*

I Hope, I Think, I Know

Words & Music by Noel Gallagher

1. They're try-ing hard— to put me in my place— and that is why— I got-

As _____ we beg _____ and steal _____ and bor - row,

life is hit and miss _____ and this, _____ I

hope, I think, _____ I know, _____ if I ev - er hear the names _____ you call, _____

_____ and if I stum - ble, catch _____ me when _____ I fall, _____

You'll never for-get my name.

D.%. al Coda

35

Verse 3:

You're trying hard to put me in my place
And that is why I gotta keep running
The future's mine and it's no disgrace
'Cos in the end your laugh means nothing.
D'you feel a little down today?
Bet you ain't got much to say
Who's gonna miss you when you're not there?
You know he don't care, you know he don't care.

As we beg and steal *etc.*

The Girl In The Dirty Shirt

Words & Music by Noel Gallagher

dan - cing with me,____ 'cos to me____ it does-n't mat - ter if your

hopes and dreams are shat-tered. When she says some - thin' she'll make me be-lieve____ in the girl____

____ who wears a dir - ty shirt, she knows ex - act - ly what she's worth to me.____

1-3.   *Repeat ad lib.*

She knows____ ex - act - ly what she's worth to me.____

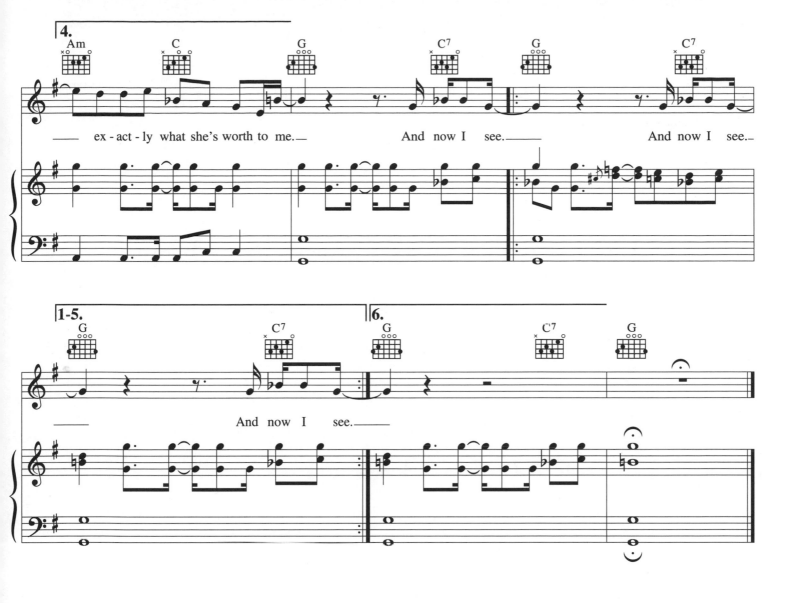

Verse 3:

If you ever find yourself inside a bubble
You've gotta make your own way home
You can call me anytime you're seeing double
Now you know you're not alone

You've got a feeling *etc.*

Fade In-Out

Words & Music by Noel Gallagher

1. Get on the rol-ler-coast - er, the fair's in town to-day.— You got-ta be— bad e - nough— to beat the brave.
(Verses 2 & 3 see block lyric)

So get on the hel-ter skel-ter, bowl in-to the fray.— You got-ta be

bad e - nough— to beat the brave.— You fade— in - out.—

You fade___ in - out,___ with - out___ ___ a doubt.___ And I don't see___ no shine___ to - day is just a day - dream. To-mor - row we'll be cast - a - way.___

in- out.___   We fade___ in- out___   With-out___ a doubt.___

And I don't see___ no shine___ to - day is just a day - dream.   To - mor-row we'll be cast a - way.

D.%. al Coda

3. So

⊕ *Coda*

You're fade_____ in - out.___   You're fade___

Verse 2:
Coming in-out of nowhere
Singin' rhapsody
You gotta be bad enough to wanna be
Sitting upside a high-chair
With the devil's refugee
Is gonna be blinded by the light that follows me

She fade in-out
She fade in-out
Without a doubt

I don't see no shine *etc.*

Verse 3:
So get on the rollercoaster
The fair's in town today
You gotta be bad enough to beat the brave
So get on the helter skelter
Step into the fray
You gotta be bad enough to beat the brave

You're fade in-out *etc.*

Don't Go Away

Words & Music by Noel Gallagher

1. Cold and frost-y morn-in', there's not a lot— to say about the things— caught— in my mind—
(Verse 2 see block lyric)

Verse 2:
Damn my situation and the games I have to play
With all the things caught in my mind.
Damn my education, I can't find the words to say
About the things caught in my mind.

I don't wanna be there *etc.*

Be Here Now

Words & Music by Noel Gallagher

1. Wash your face in the morn-ing sun,

flash your pan at the song that I'm sing-ing, touch-down bass liv-in'

on the — run, — oh make no sweat of the hole — that you're dig-ging.

2. Wrap up cold when it's warm out - side, —
(Verse 3 & 4 see block lyric)

your shit jokes re - mind — me of Dig-sy's. Be my ma - gic

car-pet___ ride,___ fly me down to ca - pi - tol ci - ty in the

Tacet 2° & 3°

sun.

Kick-in' up a storm from the day

___ that I was born, sing a song for me, one___

You bet-cha

You bet-cha

D.%. al Coda

4. So

60

⊕ *Coda*

Get a grip in - side,_____ get a grip in side,___ ___ a grip in - side,__ yeah.

Play 4 times

Verse 3:

So wash your face in the morning sun
Flash your pan at the song that I'm singing
Touch-down bass livin' on the run
Make no sweat of the hole that you're digging.

Kickin' up a storm *etc.*

Verse 4:

So wrap up cold when it's warm outside
Please sit down you make me feel giddy
Be my magic carpet ride
Fly me down to capitol city.

Been kickin' up a storm *etc.*

All Around The World

Words & Music by Noel Gallagher

1. It's a bit ear-ly in the mid-night hour for me ___ to
(Verse 2 see block lyric)

go through all ___ the things ___ that I want to be. ___

these are cra - zy days— but they make me shine.—

Time keeps roll-ing by.— All a-round the world,— you got-ta spread the word—

_____ tell 'em what you heard,— we're gon - na make a bet - ter day.

_____ All a - round the world,— you got - ta spread the word,—

na _____ na _____ na na na na na na na na _____

na na na na na na na na _____

na na na na na na na na _____

na na na na na na na na na na na na na na na na.—

Got - ta spread the word _____ tell 'em what you heard,

we're gon-na make a bet-ter day,_____ yes all a-round the world,__

you got-ta spread the word_____ tell 'em what you heard,__

you know it's gon-na be O. K.__ Yes all a-round the world__

It's gon-na be O. K.__

It's gon-na be O. K.____

It's gon-na be O. K.____ It's gon-na be O. K.____ All a-round the world__

you got - ta spread the word_____ and tell 'em what you heard,__

we're gon-na make a bet - ter day,_____ yes all a-round the world__

you got-ta spread the word_____ and tell 'em what you heard,_

you know it's gon-na be O. K.____ All a-round the world___

La la__ la la la la__ la la__

__ la la la la la.__ La la__ la

Verse 2:
What you gonna do when the walls come falling down
You never move, you never make a sound
Where you gonna swim with the riches that you found
If you're lost at sea, well I hope that you've drowned.

Take me away *etc.*

It's Gettin' Better (Man!!)

Words & Music by Noel Gallagher

1. Say _____ some - thing, shout it from the roof - tops of your head.

Make it sort of mean,_____ some - thing make me un - der -

stand or I'll for - get.____ 2. The peo - ple here on

lifes_____ beach - es wish up - on the waves that hide the sand.__
(Verse 3 see block lyric)

___ let them know that life_____ teach - es you to build a

It's get - ting bet - ter man!

Repeat 4 times ad lib.

Instrumental solo

D.%. al Coda

It's get-ting bet-ter man!

Verse 3:
Build something, build a better place and call it home
Even if it means nothing you'll never ever feel that you're alone.

Maybe the songs *etc.*

All Around The World (Reprise)

Words & Music by Noel Gallagher

Repeat ad lib. to fade

Exclusive Distributors:

Music Sales Limited, 8/9 Frith Street, London W1V 5TZ, England.

Music Sales Pty Limited, 120 Rothschild Avenue, Rosebery, NSW 2018, Australia.

Order No. AM950598

ISBN 0-7119-7037-8

Music arranged by Derek Jones & Roger Day.

Music processed by Paul Ewers Music Design.

Printed in the United Kingdom by Halstan & Co Limited, Amersham, Buckinghamshire.

Your Guarantee of Quality:

As publishers, we strive to produce every book to the highest commercial standards.

The music has been freshly engraved and, whilst endeavouring to retain the

original running order of the recorded album, the book has been carefully designed to

minimise awkward page turns and to make playing from it a real pleasure.

Particular care has been given to specifying acid-free, neutral-sized

paper made from pulps which have not been elemental chlorine bleached.

This pulp is from farmed sustainable forests and was produced with special regard for the environment.

Throughout, the printing and binding have been planned to ensure a sturdy,

attractive publication which should give years of enjoyment.

If your copy fails to meet our high standards, please inform us and we will gladly replace it.

Music Sales' complete catalogue describes thousands of titles and

is available in full colour sections by subject, direct from Music Sales Limited.

Please state your areas of interest and send a cheque/postal order for £1.50 for postage to:

Music Sales Limited, Newmarket Road, Bury St. Edmunds, Suffolk IP33 3YB.